I0640182

SIMPLE TRUTHS USED
BY GREAT SINGERS

Sarah Robinson-Duff

SIMPLE TRUTHS USED
BY GREAT SINGERS

BY
Sarah Robinson-Duff

WILDSIDE PRESS

Copyright, MCMXIX, by Oliver Ditson Company
International Copyright Secured

TO MY FIRST PUPIL,
MARY GARDEN

CONTENTS

PREFACE

It is with great hesitancy that I present to the public the series of conferences, or talks, I would better say, which I wrote and delivered before the "Palestrina Summer School of Music" during my first season in America. The appeal from many of those who have listened to them and claimed to have found help, has been so insistent, that I yield to their request, hoping perhaps to bring light and understanding to some of my fellow workers.

I have been impressed anew with the wealth of beautiful voices in the United States, as well as the native talent and receptivity of this generation of young people. The race is to the young and the strong, and nothing should be spared in our fair land to arm our youth with the best knowledge possible to attain. This seems to be a propitious time to think deeply and realize that we hold and are able to produce great ideals in art. We are giving our magnificent men to the world today that they may proclaim the "Idealism of America" and the art world should have its quota of soldiers who are working behind the lines to raise the musical standard to the pinnacle we acclaim for ourselves in other things.

As time moves on America must realize that, to a greater or less degree, she will have to depend upon her own resources in music. Our opera houses carry more and more American names on their roster, and the legitimate concert stage is well represented. The world of European musical art has deluged our country with all that is greatest and best from its wonderful storehouse, and our people have generously subscribed to their support. New lines of perfection have been reached and ideals created which we must "*carry on.*"

S. R. D.

New York, January 1, 1919.

I

BREATHING

TO me has been accorded the voice—the singing voice. Alas! What a multitude of emotions is implied in this little word of five letters! How many brilliant artists and great minds are evoked at this word! And to those of us who have had international experience of working in the art, how many sad memories of broken hearts and ruined lives come to our minds.

Why should this latter be possible? There are diverse causes and reasons from which I will choose only the most simple:

Too great haste is, unquestionably, an American characteristic, and it obtains in Europe as in America, in its most exaggerated form, among those who are contemplating a musical career. To sing, takes time; to sing as an artist takes more time, and to sing as a finished artist, takes time unlimited.

I very much fear that often when a young student starts out with the desire to become an artist, it is without any real appreciation of what the word "artist" implies, and the thought of the glitter and glamour of the stage has a far deeper influence upon his ideals than the nobility of the art he has chosen.

Too often indiscriminate praise and encouragement is given by the family and friends of these young aspirants, without any real understanding on their part of the requirements.

In Europe the knowledge of at least three languages is indispensable, and yet, the average American student arrives with a very indifferent acquaintance even with his own native tongue. But, I must here remark that for the average American girl with a mediocre education, her ability to learn a foreign language is quite unique, and I have frequently had American pupils who, while unable to speak either French or Italian well, have achieved a flawless diction in those languages.

A second impediment to good progress is their lack of any real musical education. Harmony is an unopened book, and the piano has very often been equally neglected. The local teacher from whom they have received their first instruction, while perfectly conscientious in her work, has failed to give them the first principle upon which to produce a voice. And what do you believe the first principle to be—breath? Yes, breath.

As one of the great old Italian masters says, to produce a beautiful singing voice there are three essentials: "breath, again breath, and still again *more* breath." And I am inclined to agree with him.

When we hear a great orchestra, violinist, 'cellist, pianist or singer, what is our first impression?—the beautiful legato, sostenuto tones produced.

I so often have pupils say to me: "How do they do it, how do they get that beautiful line in singing? I have studied long and conscientiously, and I have only occasionally produced it."

The reason is never far to seek. It will usually be found in the lack of *good breathing*, and it is with this subject that I propose we shall begin our work today.

Singing is an exact science, and if presented in a clear, concise manner, should not be so difficult to understand. As a matter of fact, the average pupil has a very imperfect understanding of this science, which is due to two well-known causes. First, the pupil becomes intimidated at the effort made to make him understand from a scientific physical standpoint, and fails to grasp the great help he would have, were he able to analyze and know the reason for his faults as well as his good points. Unless one is master of this problem, the only other principle which can aid in the singing voice, is sensation. But, how can one arrive at having this sensaation become *an established principle?* I often have a soprano, a beginner, we will say, make an exquisite tone, at which I remark, "That is a perfect tone, emitted in a perfect manner; now take the next one in exactly the same manner." Almost without exception, the next note is quite another production, a bad one. When I tell her this she says, "But why, Mrs. Duff? I took my breath in the same way, and did identically the same thing that I did in the last note."

"Did you have the same sensation?"

"No, it did not feel quite as easy."

"Well, how did the first one feel, where did you feel it?"

"Why, I did not feel anything, it just came."

There, my friends, lies all the secret. It does not just come—there are no chances in singing—you must know *what* you do and *why* you do it. It is based upon inviolable laws and you must master these laws.

The approved method of breathing, adopted by the greatest artists, is the diaphragmatic, or, as it is sometimes badly named, abdominal breathing. The only way in which the abdomen is concerned is the sympathy that exists and that we necessarily feel between the diaphragm and muscles of the abdomen.

You are of course aware that the lungs lie on the muscle of the diaphragm; which is convex in shape. It forms the floor of the thorax or

[7]

chest, and at the same time serves as a roof to the abdomen. The lungs are spongy in texture, and when breath is inhaled they expand very much as a dry sponge in a tub of water.

Make the diaphragmatic breathing the most pronounced as it will give the smoothest control, being the most powerful of the breathing muscles, using the lateral breathing very slightly to increase the quantity, but *never sacrificing* the diaphragmatic to the lateral breathing, thus securing the greatest capacity with the control vested in the most powerful muscles.

When the breath is nearly exhausted and the diaphragm contracted, to complete the expulsion of the remaining breath the pillars of the diaphragm are brought into play.

This is known as the singer's last resort.

The diaphragm should not be drawn in, or at least very little in taking breath, and the abdomen never. The chest should be slightly raised, but not too much. Exercises for expansion of the chest are invaluable. You must be able to control your breath as long as you wish to finish your tone or phrase, and it is only when the apparent pressure of the diaphragm and chest stops that your breath is finished, and then it is the pressure is slowly relaxed and the chest at the end sinks very gradually.

Breath control must be constant; take neither too much nor too little. You must have enough to take a big long phrase, and when you want to sing piano, do not be too niggardly, nor again too extravagant.

The great French baritone, Monsieur Renaud, once told me that he was floundering about for years, trying to adjust the difference which existed between his breath and singing tone, and at last he found the key in the conservation of energy. Take all the breath you need quietly and slowly and keep it without stiffening anywhere. Complete relaxation of the entire body is your first principle. Breathing is often likened to organ bellows and can be controlled in the same manner. The control must not cease even at the end of the phrase or note or period of expiration, and the singer must always finish with a little in reserve.

One should breathe through the

nose with a closed mouth, and thus fill the lungs, and the upper ribs naturally respond, thereby forcing the breath against the chest where it is held unconsciously. Chest and diaphragm, the closed epiglottis, all form a supply chamber for the breath. I would especially warn all teachers of singing against using, or rather abusing, the so-called lateral breathing, most pernicious in its results. In place of having a soft cushion on which to place the voice, only an empty chasm is produced by this latter manner of breathing.

Another valuable adjunct for the controlled emission of breath is the raised palate. This has a tendency to uncover the tongue in the back of the mouth and thereby prepare a road through which the breath finds a smooth and even egress, instead of being held or forced back upon the vocal cords. When the latter occurs, as it all too frequently does, the tone produced is hard and shakes and is unmusical. We often find singers in their desire to have breath support holding the breath by stiffening the diaphragm or the muscles of the larynx, and thus depriving the tone of all elasticity and floating quality.

The understanding of the breath, its relation to epiglot, palate and tongue, is only the knowledge of the breath regulators which puts into your hands an indisputable weapon. As soon as the breath leaves the larynx, it is divided; one part may press toward the palate, the other toward the cavities of the head. This occurs from deepest base to highest soprano, unvaryingly, and without regard to sex. Its difference depends only upon the size and strength of the vocal organs through which the breath flows and the skill with which it is used. *Le point de depart*, the seat of the breath, as well as the resonating surfaces, are always the same. The breath must never be held back, but always expelled in a regular, even manner, and as you ascend the scale, in a more and more powerful form. When told to always breathe through the nose, many pupils take exception to this, and say that they cannot do it, that it is too labored, and that it takes too much time.

In the beginning I admit it is rather annoying to do so, and oftentimes causes one to sing out of time; but

after awhile when the muscles have
become thoroughly limbered through
use, then one can get the breath much
more quickly, and the more one can
breathe through the nose, the better
it is. But, naturally, when one is an
accomplished artist, and singing in
opera, or even songs, one is often
compelled to breathe with an open
mouth.

Lilli Lehman once told me that she
used the closed mouth breathing as
often as she could, for she found that
she sang with a fresher voice and for
a longer time. As a matter of fact,
when breathing with closed mouth,
neither the cold air not dust can
strike the vocal passages.

You may possibly know of the use
of the candle in practising breathing.
Nothing is better, to my mind, than

this exercise performed daily and year after year. If the candle flickers the breath and the singing is bad. This was an absolute test employed by the *Bel Cantists* and if the flame flickered the tone was pronounced imperfect.

It may seem strange to you if I say that you are each and every one capable of finding a method of breathing by which you can best express your art thoughts, and with the hints I have given you it should not be difficult of realization, for you must ever remember that the body depends upon the mind for its inspiration, in both senses. It is not after all the *amount* of breath you take, but it is the *control* you have over it. And with control of breath comes control of your acts; and with a mind well-

poised and calm, the achievement of
a good breath is a foregone conclu-
sion. Thus we see how closely allied
are the simple laws of nature, and
it is only when we become confused
and troubled that we fail. Ask any
artist of great achievement what he
or she considers their greatest asset,
and they will unfalteringly tell you,
"My breath control." Annie Louise
Cary told me that she never stepped
her foot upon the stage, even after
years of tremendous success, that
her legs did not tremble so that she
feared they would give out from
under her, and it was only after she
had sung a few phrases and found
her breath control, that she gained
her self-possession and could go on
with her performance.

I could cite you examples unnum-

bered of artists who have met with
great success, or failed unutterably,
where in each case they have been
able to trace their success or failure
to breath conditions.

II

TONE PLACING

OUR first talk has to do with breathing, which is the foundation principle of all good singing. You cannot speak without breath, and if our breath stops, material life stops; nor can you sing without breath. To the untutored vocal mind, I think it can never, even in a vague way, comprehend this marvelous sympathy and direct co-operation between breath and tone.

What produces a vocal tone?

The vibration of the air on the vocal chords.

Where are these delicate, and so often abused, vocal chords? Where do they lie?

They are attached to each side of the larynx and the action of the breath passing through, sets the chords in vibration, and the preparation of the intermediary canal between throat and lips is the determining factor which produces either a beautiful, mediocre, or thoroughly bad tone.

The first essential, after a good breath has been acquired, is to gain complete relaxation of the jaw. And I wonder if you realize what that means. Nine people out of ten, especially those speaking the English language, have an almost rigid, or, as I call it, iron jaw.

In twenty-five years of teaching the singing voice, I have never yet found what you would call a naturally relaxed jaw and tongue. Oftentimes, when one can relax thoroughly the jaw without singing, the moment one attempts to produce a vocal tone, the jaw and tongue become absolutely rigid, and hence cut off the supply of breath. It closes the throat, and the only possible *appui* is that furnished by the iron jaw. Sometimes, pupils will have a certain amount of relaxation of tongue and jaw on the lower tones and medium; but as soon as they feel they have to take a high note, a certain nervous contraction takes place, and fear overpowers and weakens the breath supply; and the sensation that they must have support somewhere causes them to stiffen the jaw and depend upon that.

I can be in the Metropolitan Opera House with my back turned to the stage, listening to a delightful performance, and if some one sings even one note in this manner, I recognize it at once. All freedom disappears from the tone and it has a strident, hard sound.

I feel, after all my long years of experience in teaching singing, that I cannot sufficiently impress upon your minds the importance of perfect relaxation of jaw and tongue.

This is a principle I have insisted upon in my work which has produced excellent results. In fact it gained for me in Paris the soubriquet *Chirurgien de la voix* (Surgeon of the voice).

How to achieve this is, naturally, the next question that arises. Few people, unless they have been trained to have "power through repose," can at will call on their muscles, and yet, such should be the case

I could give you pages upon the physical, metaphysical, and psychic forces as they act upon these organs, but it is going to be my effort to be as concise and simple as possible in all that I say to you, and try and not cloud the issue in any way by resorting to the use of too many technical terms. I believe this to be the reason why so little real benefit has ever been achieved by students, in the perusal of the multitudinous books on singing, given to the world not only by learned men, but by some of the world's acknowledged greatest artists, whose life-long practical experience and deep study have made each step perfectly defined in their own consciousness, but when they attempt to give it to others, simplicity seems to leave them and they do not make it clear.

Too many technical terms confuse rather than aid the young students, and yet, the master mind who is directing their studies must be so imbued with the beauty and sacred duty of his task, that he can evoke at pleasure those points which are most essential.

First,—breathe. Take a long, quiet and relaxed breath, and you will find this has already given you a more relaxed jaw; then place the palm of your hand under your jaw and un-hinge the jaw just by the ear and let it *drop* into your hand. Don't make the mistake of putting effort into relaxation, that is the cardinal sin of all beginners. When we ask for complete relaxation, their very desire to achieve it and give us what we want, causes them to try so hard that their effort defeats their aim.

Constant relaxation of the jaw should be practised in your dressing-room; when you are seated before your mirror; when you are traveling; and best of all, when you are sleepy and want to yawn.

Yawn sleepily, and when you do, place your finger just under your ear; then try to analyze your sensations, and see how your tongue feels; how and where it lies; and also what is the position of the soft palate.

I would almost go so far as to say that if a person cannot acquire a supple jaw and tongue, they had better give up trying to learn to sing.

If the jaw becomes perfectly relaxed and the breath under complete control, it is rare that the tongue does not follow suit. But there are some cases where students have acquired a perfectly relaxed jaw and the tongue still remains an insufferable barrier. The same principle of relaxation applies to the tongue that applies to the jaw, and if you can absolutely relax the root of the tongue, and let the tip of the tongue lie softly against the lower teeth, you will rarely have difficulty with it.

If the tongue is perfect for singing, it should have a furrow in the middle, which is least prominent in the lowest tones, and sometimes in the highest head tones completely disappears. If the furrow becomes habitual with a singer, you may be certain that he or she is singing entirely upon their breath, and this keeps the large part of the tongue out of the throat, and as the sides necessarily are high, it leaves a trough or passage for a perfect tone.

In my early days of studying the voice I was made to go through hours of torture by introducing into the mouth a spoon or some foreign substance to make the tongue lie flat. The more I endeavored to hold the tongue down, religiously following my Professor's instructions, the more rebellious my tongue became and the shorter my temper.

One day when in my dentist's chair he asked me how I could ever hope to sing with such a stiff tongue. His explanation to me of the relation of tongue, jaw and diaphragm, was the first rift in the clouds to send me on my way of investigation. I shall always look upon it as a "red letter day," for from that moment my mission became more clear, and with study and patience I have evolved my principles for work on the singing voice.

The tongue lies flattest in the low tones because the larynx is in its lowest position. Just as we feel the resonance of the low tones in the chest we feel the medium tones higher, and the top notes in the head, which is due to the different positions of the larynx. The tongue, as I have told you, should always lie easily, hence naturally, against the lower teeth, and it is the strongest factor after your lips in pronunciation and good diction. You take, for instance, the letter *L* in the words *la-le-li* and if you put the tongue back of the upper teeth to pronounce the consonant *L* and let it fall immediately back of your lower teeth again you will find that your tongue and jaw are relaxed, and that you are holding and supporting your tone entirely by the breath. You will then know that delightful sensation which comes to the artist when he feels the current of air passing unobtruded until it reaches the lips, and then bursts forth into a joyful, relaxed tone. And until one has achieved this key, singing never can be an art; and rarely a joy.

In the earlier years of my teaching singing, I used to watch the great artists and realized that their tongue never really left the teeth, and that it was frequently turned up in front, resting against the upper teeth. This was especially true of Édouard and Jean De Reszké, Melba, and our own great Caruso indulges in the same thing.

It puzzled me for a very long time, and it was only after years of deepest research, talking and discussing with these artists, that I discovered the wonderful value of this in singing.

It is much to be regretted that the student body cannot be made to realize the importance of the foundation work which appears to them *drudgery*. As much as possible this work should not be *made* drudgery, but rather the understanding should be borne in upon their minds that it is the "golden key" they are forging which will either open or close the door of all future success.

All the truly great artists will tell you that it is absolutely essential to practise before a mirror until you have become complete master of these members—tongue and jaw; and yet, I fancy my experience is not different from others, and I find it one of my most difficult principles to obtain.

There is a peculiar psychological something which transpires in the human mind when one finds oneself looking at one's reflection in a mirror in the presence of another person, and I am told by my pupils that when they look at themselves, they cannot concentrate as well.

I have often wished that I could find a mirror that would give the reflection to just above the *fausse nasal*, and so eliminate eyes, hair, etc.

We have dealt now progressively with *breath, jaw, tongue*; and now we arrive at the lips which have the power to caress or mangle the tone when it arrives at the door of egress.

Nothing is more delightful and positively comforting than to hear good diction, to be able to sit back and listen to a story borne to us on its tone chariot.

Mme. Calvé once told me that for years she practised the lips and the muscles of the *fausse nasal* two hours a day unceasingly. I have found very little benefit derived from practising anything spasmodically; and with the power to work systematically and intelligently comes also a realizing sense of the beauty and sincerity of art and intolerance of mediocrity, which is the greatest inspiration to the development of the spiritual ideal in work as well as art.

Can you do a thing well if you don't like to do it?

I cannot.

Can you accomplish anything if you don't like to do it well?

No one can.

There can be just as high an ideal put into the accomplishment of technique as there can be in the rendition of a great operatic aria, and the person who does not place this ideal in the foundation which he or she lays for their building, will find that something always lacks. They think that they have arrived at a certain point and, alas! when the moment of realization comes, fulfilment is not what they believed it would be, and the still small voice says, "Oh, if I had only been a little more serious, if I had only understood a little better what was required when I began, I could have achieved great things."

Let us all remember that we only pass once this way, and whether it is the study of breath, relaxation of jaw, or tongue, or the interpretation of some sublime aria, let us bring to it the best we have, and we shall receive accordingly.

This was forcibly brought to my mind when I was a very young girl. I studied one winter the history of art under a remarkable teacher. She had passed a great deal of time in Europe and had been a profound student of the old masters. She was a woman of great wealth and had thus been able to provide herself with every adjunct in the way of pictures, books, etc. I was going to Europe the next year, and I remem-

ber so distinctly when she turned to
me one day as I had had a particu-
larly good lesson, and made this
remark: "Remember, my child, that
you will bring back with you exactly
in proportion to what you carry
with you." This has been impressed
upon my mind over and over again
by actual experience.

———

Allow me to revert once more to the
great necessity of relaxation in all
you do, and of a well-defined knowledge of each step taken, that you
may have a perfect structure whose
architect you are. Your art must not
control you, but you must control
your art, and the key to this, as far
as we have gone in the art of singing,
is based upon three fundamental
principles: *Breath, Jaw and Tongue.*

III

TONE PLACING
(*Continued*)

That we may have no deception
nor misunderstanding in our work,
let us recall to mind the two pre-
ceding lessons: the first on breath—
diaphragmatic breathing, second
flexibility of the jaw, third, *souplesse*
of tongue, and fourth agility of the
lips.

These four cardinal points well-
established in our minds, we can pro-
ceed to the form of the mouth and
the attack of the tone. The form of
the mouth in different persons must
essentially vary, just as the shape of
the mouth varies in different indi-
viduals. For the contralto and mezzo-

soprano voices, it is wise to have the mouth in a rather dome-shaped form in exercises, with the lips slightly advanced, very much as a man playing the cornet or any other mouth instrument.

Monsieur Lucien Muratore once told me that when he was a boy he played the saxophone in a local orchestra, and he had found it of inestimable value in his singing, because of the strength his lips had gained.

The high light soprano or coloratura singers are inclined to have the mouth in a more smiling position, but for the shape of the mouth an exact rule is impossible, for the reasons I have already defined. Hence, what I have said upon this point only is submitted as a possible guide, but each individual pupil is entitled to personal consideration in this matter.

By closing off the throat from the cavities of the head, the chest voice is produced, the lowest range of all the voice. This closing of the throat from the head cavities is brought about by raising the pillars of the fauces, familiarly known to us as the pharynx. As we go up the scale and the soft palate is raised higher and higher, behind the nose, the pillars of the fauces are lowered, and this provides an unimpeded road for the sending of the breath to the head cavities. The breath arriving there fills the nose, forehead and head cavities, and produces what is known as the head voice.

When the soft palate is raised high in the back, a stream of breath, however small, must be forced back, behind and above the fauces, first into the nose, later into the forehead and the cavities of the head. This forms the overtones, head tones, which must vibrate with every note.

It is very interesting to note how these overtones assert themselves in the different voices. You will be more sensitive to their presence in the top notes, but they should exist in all, and the experienced artists will tell you how religiously they try to guard and cultivate these overtones.

This is the most striking feature as the voice goes more and more into place, and always adds not only to the carrying quality but to the purity and beauty of the voice. When one sings a single note, one can give it much more resonance than one can in singing scales.

To attack a tone one must have a focused pivotal point to which to direct the breath, and this, after all, is what produces the tone. Many people who are not students of the voice or physiology, firmly believe that the tones are attacked in the throat. This is an error. Alas, many poor unfortunates do sing in their throats, but the proper office for this much abused organ *is simply that of a passageway.*

I do not pretend to say that the correct development of the muscles and different organs of the throat, as well as its form and elasticity, are not all great factors in producing a beautiful tone, but here again comes in the necessity for complete relaxation, and this gives an adequate and intelligent reason for the length of time required to really sing well.

You do not expect an athlete to lift five hundred pounds the first day, but, on the contrary, he begins by lifting very little at a time. He never allows a day to pass in which he does not work, and hence increases the weight he lifts as he gains control of his muscles. But how different the singing pupil, who after two or three months of more or less irregular work cannot understand why he has not already accomplished what it has taken others years to attain.

If one would only begin this work with a spirit of absolute simplicity, almost humility, I may say, the first law of relaxation would have been achieved.

I should like to call your attention to the use or *abuse*, of the *attack of the glottis*. This is caused by an abrupt or harsh closing of the vocal cords. A closing together or clicking together, which, if persisted in for a long enough period, will result in great injury to the cords. In some instances, after a certain length of time, they refuse to close in the middle and thus a breathy tone is emitted. Again they will close in the middle and become separated at each end. The most pernicious result of all, however, is when a corn or nodule forms on the cords as a result of this constant friction. The glottis attack is responsible for the loss of many voices, even the most robust seem unable to resist this harsh treatment. It is not infrequent that artists who have made their debut in a brilliant manner soon disappear from public view or sink into mediocrity, and this unfortunate condition emanates frequently from the attack of the glottis.

I was studying with Madam Marchesi at the same time that Madam X was a student. In fact, I was present at her debut in Brussels. The voice was wonderfully crystalline, pure in quality, and very brilliant; and the world needs no word of mine to tell of her gigantic success, but, what you perhaps do not know is that at the end of Madam X's first season, she lost her voice. She attributed it to great fatigue, and went to London to consult with Sir Morrell Mackenzie, the well-known throat specialist. You will remember that he was the man who was sent for to go to the Crown Prince Frederick when he was suffering from the

malady which cost him his life—
cancer of the throat.

Dr. Mackenzie sent Madam X to
Ems to take the waters for her throat,
and after a cure of twenty-one days,
she came back to London for another
examination.

She was again sent away for still
another cure, at the expiration of
which time she was pronounced
perfectly well.

The following autumn Madam X
came for the first time to America to
sing in opera with Abbey & Grau.
Shortly after arriving she was again
suffering from some throat disturb-
ance and she consulted Dr. Holbrook
Curtis. Dr. Curtis, after a thorough
examination pronounced it a case of
a corn on the vocal cords. Naturally, Madam X protested that it was

impossible. He asked her if she had ever had any throat difficulty. "No, never." The Doctor then asked her to reflect very carefully and see if she could not remember some time when she had suffered from her throat. After a moment, she said, "Why, at the end of my season last spring, my voice was very fatigued and Dr. Mackenzie sent me to a cure; but simply because of fatigue." Dr. Curtis then suggested that she cable Dr. Mackenzie and ask him just what had been her difficulty, and the answer came back: "Corn on vocal cords."

For some years it was said that Madam X had written a book upon the attack of the glottis introducing this incident, which she would publish after the death of Madam

Marchesi. Poor Madam passed away
some years ago, and to my knowledge
no such book has been published.
But I do know that Madam X put
herself into the hands of Dr. Curtis,
and through his cure and the use of
some of the exercises that he has
given in his admirable book, she completely reposed and regained her
voice, and when I heard her in Paris
a year ago last May give a gala
performance of Bohème, I still found
her voice the purest and most beautiful in the world.

I know that she was very much
troubled and worried over the fact
that Madam Marchesi taught the
glottis attack. On the occasion of her
first visit to Chicago I was living and
teaching there at the time. I had
lunched and dined with Madam X

several times with friends, when, finally, one day, she sent for me to come to her room—she was staying at the Auditorium Hotel, where I was living. After half an hour's conversation concerning friends, the opera, generalities, etc., she got up, went to the piano, struck middle A and said "Sing that tone for me." I was rather surprised, but did as she told me. Then she played three or four upper medium notes, and then one or two head notes. When I had finished singing, all she said was "Thank God, I was afraid to hear you sing for fear you were teaching the attack of the glottis."

Her loyalty to Madam Marchesi was very beautiful; she recognized her tremendous talent and great musicianship, besides being unceasingly grateful to her for what she did for her while she was studying and before she made her debut.

I myself feel great delicacy in criticizing Madam Marchesi's work, for she was certainly one of the greatest geniuses of her day, and the only possible fault one could find is her use of the attack of the glottis, and the division of the voice into three registers: chest, medium and head.

This was also used by Garcia, but it leads to many exaggerations and false ideas.

The so-called chest tone is now obsolete, and when one hears it, it is offensive even to the uncultivated ear.

Each tone, from lowest chest to highest head, should be taken in a line which never varies, that is to say, one should not be able to distinguish when one passes from one so-called register to another.

Madam Nordica once said to me that she felt her highest head and her lowest chest note at exactly the same place, that is to say, on the lips, or *fausse nasal*.

The use of the *fausse nasal* is very valuable, and one should really visibly feel each note in this place. When one has succeeded in doing this, then the line is achieved.

The nasal resonance, intelligently used, is also valuable if thoroughly understood; but used with a closed throat, it becomes so pinched that it does not have the desired effect. Caruso often sings with this nasal quality and I know that he uses it frequently in practise. With beginners, I

find it works much better to precede
the vowel by a consonant, presumably
L, M or *N.* This obviates, usually,
the throat or glottis attack. I have
rarely had a pupil come to me for
work who does not indulge in this
false attack.

In placing the tone on the lips one
has the sensation as if the air came
up the back of the throat, and first
forms an arch for the medium and
upper notes; and one feels the arch
more and more pronounced for the
upper and head notes, although *Le
point de depart* is exactly the same.
And yet each note has its own little
niche and one can physically feel it.
I often liken this niche to a pocket on
a pool table. If you have aimed well
and measured your distance correctly, the ball will softly roll into place,

otherwise it dances about on the edge.
It is the same with the voice and the
perfectly placed tone, and they are all
too rare.

IV

EVENING UP THE VOICE

IN our last lesson we gave much
thought to the direction of the
tone, and now, today, I propose
to consider somewhat the evening up
of the voice.

Many of the old professors divided
the voice into three registers,—*chest,
medium* and *head*.

What is a vocal register?

It is a series or succession of tones
which are produced by certain positions of the vocal cords, larynx,
tongue, and palate.

In reality, every voice does have
these registers, but they are not
always used. It is quite frequent
among beginners to find two of them

connected; the third is usually much weaker, and often does not exist at all. It is very rare to find a voice that you may say is naturally equalized throughout its registers. The question arises, "Has Nature provided these registers?" Lilli Lehman says, "No." Regarding them as unnatural she explains their origin as follows:–

It may be said that they are created through long years of speaking in the vocal range that is easiest to the person, or in one adopted by imitation, which then becomes a fixed habit. If this is coupled with a natural and proper working of the muscles of the vocal organs, it may become the accustomed range, strong in comparison with others, and form a register by itself. This fact would naturally be appreciated only by singers.

If, on the other hand, the muscles

are wrongly employed in speaking, not only the range of voice generally used, but the whole voice as well, may be made to sound badly. So, in every voice, or another range may be stronger or weaker; and this is, in fact, almost always the case, since mankind speaks and sings in the pitch easiest or most accustomed, without giving thought to the proper position of the organs in relation to each other; and people are rarely made to pay attention as children to speaking clearly and in an agreeable voice.

On the contrary, Madam Marchesi always claimed that the voice was by nature divided into three registers, thoroughly pronounced, one from the other—chest, medium and head. Naturally, when the voice became placed, the exact passing from one register to another was eliminated by blending together passage notes. She gave as a reason for this the fact that the larynx was in its lowest position for the chest notes; mounted as one goes up the scale until it reached the highest position—the head notes. My own experience has taught me that it is confusing for a pupil to think of registers, and a much more simple method is to blend one into the other gradually without their knowing when they are passing.

In almost all voices difficulty is experienced on the so-called passage notes. With sopranos it usually comes between B and C in the middle registers; or E and F in the upper medium. Contraltos more often experience great difficulty between E and G (first and second lines, treble staff) or B and C (third line and third space, treble staff).

As the upper voice more readily acquires easier control of the overtones, I find it practicable, in nine cases out of ten, to have pupils begin their vocal exercises on the upper notes, and work downward, and never from the very low voice up, until a certain and complete understanding of placing the middle notes has been acquired.

If a beginner is given a scale or group of notes, beginning on *B* or *C* below the staff, he immediately begins to think low, which often creates a throaty back quality.

If these notes can be placed high enough in thought, they will have their quota of overtones, and be beautiful notes. It has always been such a pleasure to hear Litvinne and Destinn sing in this part of the voice.

They give to these notes all the warmth and velvet without sacrificing any of their brilliancy, and a complete line is preserved; and you hear the highest head and the lowest chest tones taken with equal precision. I do not need to tell you how rare this is among singers.

In placing the voice all registers should be made to blend imperceptibly. If one forces, one is certain to pay the price; and the voice becomes very defective.

You will sometimes hear singers—sopranos, we will say—who force their chest voice; then you may be sure that the medium will be weakened; and oftentimes, I have heard sopranos sing full chest voice up to A and B flat. These singers, needless to say, rarely have any head voice.

Then come days of tears and bitter disappointment, for when you take the chest away from the medium, the muscles have been so strained that the notes are perfectly hollow. And it takes days and months using vocal massage before any real tone will come. Nine cases out of ten, the weakness always remains, at least in thought.

The head voice, when it is thoroughly appreciated, is one of the most valuable, as well as one of the most cherished possessions of a singer. A beautiful head voice, correctly understood, is sometimes the saviour of a middle register; but, on the contrary, if a middle register is forced, one can never hope to have really beautiful top notes.

And thus, you see, how interdependent the voice is, one part upon the other, and how absolutely necessary that each step be directed by a master mind, which knows in advance the effect of each exercise given, upon the different organs and muscles.

I much fear that I have not the reputation of being very amiable and agreeable in my work; for I am very exacting, especially with beginners.

I have often had people say to me: "I should so much like to have my daughter study with you, but I suppose you don't like to bother with beginners, and then, too, your lessons are so very expensive. I know a very nice young teacher who only charges two dollars a lesson; now, if my daughter could only begin with her and then you would take her a little later—that would be charming."

I always say: "By all means have your daughter study with this teacher, but don't ask me to take her afterwards. It is too hard work to undo the bad work she will have done."

The most important work in any art is the foundation, and then is the time when one should have the best lessons. It is never the size of the voice that is its determining qualification for success. Many times a tone which seems to the person themselves small, will possess a far greater carrying quality than the tone which vibrates enormously inside one's own head. The tone must have projection to have success.

Placing the tones in the masque of

the face or on the teeth, as we sometimes say, is often misunderstood;
and the tone is thin and without
roundness or depth. This is *always*
true if these tones are not supported
by the breath.

When you are told to support a
tone by the breath, what is the mental picture you create?

I am almost certain that if you will
carefully analyze your sensation you
will find a rigidity of all the muscles
controlling the breath and vocal
organs. In nine cases out of ten this
is true.

Recall to mind once again, please,
that the lungs lie on the muscle of
the diaphragm. When you have
taken a long quiet breath, then relax
and attack the note with the *appogio*
or breath support. This is what

should give the impetus to the tone,
and it is from there that the attack
comes which produces the beautiful
velvety note. In order to have this
attack pure and true one must open
the throat. If the *appogio* is the
receptacle of the voice, the throat is
its issue, and it is useless to attempt
to emit or give out a note if the
throat is not sufficiently opened to
insure a free passage.

This emission of voice is frequently
a remarkable substitute for so-called
temperament, whereas no temperament, no matter how rich and vital,
can ever completely replace a beautiful tone.

Another cause of imperfect tone
production is due to not making intelligent use of all the resonators
nature has provided. A singer can

only have control of her voice by practising the vocal gymnastics indicated daily. The mastering of all these muscles must become subconscious. In the beginning, one must scientifically know, and then one must both know and feel. Practice in this manner never fatigues the voice, and the more one can do of this kind of work, the more beautiful the voice becomes.

There are certain singers who use too much head tone throughout the voice, and this produces a white voice and invariably is first heard in the middle register. This white middle register, so much in use today, has just that element of truth in it which makes it a dangerous tool in the hands of the inexperienced.

Some well-known singers at times

produce in the middle range such a
white open tone that it ceases almost
to remain a tone, and becomes a
singing, speaking tone.

Again, if the middle register is kept
too dark, it becomes difficult to advance to the upper medium and head
voice. This gradual advancing of the
voice, and careful adjustment of each
note can only be acquired by patience
on the part of the pupil, and complete
understanding by the teacher whose
trained ear accustoms her to hear
the slightest variation.

Very often this white quality as used
by some opera singers has, I believe,
been brought about through trying
to give expression to certain senti-
ments. The mind is the seat of all
sentiment, and its expression in singing depends upon the power to color

with vocal brushes, in the form of vocal technique.

The farther we go from the heart of nature, the farther we go from correct and simple expression. I have somewhere read that the power of sustained breath means power of sustained tone—which is nothing but *sustained thought made audible.*

If you discuss the culture of the voice with the ordinary critic, he will tell you that singers are as a class not overburdened with brains—as a matter of fact they have just as much gray matter as other people, but they do not always make use of what they have. I go so far as to say that anyone with health, good ear, great love of the art, and willingness to listen and work, can be made to sing.

V

VOCALIZING

O UR foundation principles once established, we arrive at a moment when these must be put into practice. Shall we take a cursory glance over the previous lessons and see what these principles are.

First—*diaphragmatic breathing.*

Second—*relaxation* of *tongue* and *jaw;* position of the lips; and shape of the mouth; and now we must put all these into action through the medium of properly applied exercises. I have found in teaching that it is better for beginners to precede the vowel by a consonant, preferably *L* or *M*, to avoid the so much dreaded attack of the glottis. I believe the *L* especially useful since it involves a gymnastic exercise for the tongue, and at the same time divides the resonance on the teeth. To have the exact result, one must be certain that the throat is open, the tongue relaxed, and the jaw absolutely dead; or as Mme. Litvinne says, *Chantez comme une imbecile*—(Sing like an imbecile)—and this is not far from right.

Do not undertake long scales and difficult exercises in the beginning, but rather be content with taking the single note, using the attack of *La*. When this has achieved a medium of facility, add *Le* and *Lee*. Once this is understood (not accomplished)—for it takes months to arrive at having this really correct, then do groups of these notes, and so on until you have acquired an octave. By this you must have become convinced of the necessity of having your breath support your tones in order to produce the legato quality without which all singing is faulty and uninteresting.

Intervals now claim our attention, and we begin with an interval of a third and then pass consecutively to fourths, fifths, sixths and sevenths, until we arrive at the octave. When you are to sing an octave, no matter in what register you may be, it is not the top note that should be your pre-occupation, but rather the first note. At best an octave has a perfectly mathematical prescribed distance of eight tones. If your first note is back, down, or out of place, your top note cannot be good. If, on the contrary, when you take your first note, you have carefully thought out and measured your distance mentally, you will have taken for your first note very nearly as high an arch in position as you need for your top note. When you descend to take the lower note, do not swallow it, but leaving everything relaxed, and thinking forward and up, you will have kept the cavities so open that the tone will have its proper overtones, and hence be a beautiful note.

With the voice that is virgin pure and untouched, all these principles are comparatively simple to instill; but, when one has worked, studied and sung in the wrong way for a period of time, the muscles have

become so strongly developed that
to make one give up this old set of
muscles and cultivate the new ones—
is often very trying to both pupil and
professor.

In fact, none except those who have
patience, intelligence and endurance
should undertake it. I would recommend in practice that all exercises be
done chromatically, or by half tones.

I have insisted very strongly upon
physical relaxation, and now I must
lay equal stress upon mental relaxation. Never go to a teacher unless
you have perfect faith in him. If
you have, then become a piece of
putty and let him mould you as he
will.

Mary Garden, in sending a pupil to
me, said to her: "Go to Mrs. Duff,
study with her; she will make you

sing, but only if you *follow her unquestioningly*.

It is impossible to have any results in teaching if hidden in some recess of the pupil's mind there remains either doubt or indecision. If the teacher's arguments and principles do not appeal to your judgment and understanding, then don't study with him. Perhaps, after all, you have not the requisite talent for work. Again, possibly, you are both very talented and equally serious, but your natures are not in accord. Under these conditions do not go on.

When the first series of intervals have been studied, follow it up with the practice of the arpeggios, always beginning your phrases with the high thought, and as you ascend, we will say on *La*, for instance, in the medium take more of an *O* sound, and for the very top notes let it become almost *OO*.

Adelina Patti once told me that in the run after the trill in the beginning of the Waltz Song in *Faust*, she always made her trill and first notes on an open *Ah*, and finished on an *OO*. If you will do it this way, you will find it simplifies matters very much.

Clara Louise Kellogg told me that she had placed all her head notes on an open English *A* or *Ah*. If you will do this exercise, you will soon understand why. The soft palate and the back of the throat are lifted very high. When you sing a single note in any part of the voice, it is easier to give more power to it than in an ascending scale, or a series of ascending tones.

The breath must never be held back at any time, and the higher the tone the more numerous are the vibrations: For the low notes of all voices the resonance is created by the projection of the breath against the palate, in which instance the fauces are stretched to their fullest extent. This allows very little air to pass to the cavities of the head which gives you a logical explanation of this established law.

In the descending scale, try to hold the form and position you have had for your top note.

Nordica said that as she went up the scale, she thought down; as she went down, she thought up. Books on vocalization will always provide you with scale exercises introducing every degree of difficulty. It is always better to do at least one long slow scale a day in a very sustained quiet manner, and then afterward do as many for agility as you like, avoiding religiously the desire to force.

I counsel all vocalizing in *mezzo-voce* and *piano*, at least until the muscles have become so trained that the scale goes, as it were, of itself. Beginners are so apt to force, and if asked to *crescendo* on an ascending scale, before the voice is pretty well placed, I have found it hazardous.

When I was a child in the State of Maine, they used to have embossed mottoes with inscriptions like this: "Welcome," "God Bless Our Home," etc. I should like to have the rooms of teachers and students embossed with mottoes of this order:

"Patience," "Don't Hurry," "Relax and Take Your Time," "Don't Force."

If students were only privileged to talk with and know more of the method of practising employed by the great artists, they would be much more amenable to the demands made upon them by conscientious and intelligent teachers.

It has been my happy privilege to know many of the greatest artists of this epoch, and I have found one unfailing principle established in their work—*never* practice in full voice— always *piano* or *mezzo-voce*. The temptation is very great to the student when the voice is developing, and becoming more beautiful in quality and greater in volume, to wish to hear his own voice and so sing in full tone. Nothing can be more fatal.

I cannot tell you how much I wish that any word of mine could save even one seeker after the truth in singing from the many pitfalls that surround them.

Let your brain work before your voice does; for once done wrong you have strengthened a bad habit, and *vice versa.* I believe that the most beautiful voices in the world today are in America, but untrained minds and characters are often the undoing of this to me the greatest of God's gifts.

We, as teachers, have it largely in our power to aid materially in the development and training of the mind. I have often felt that there was almost no other relation in life that evoked more gratitude and affection than being able to help one to learn to sing; and as this can only be acquired after long consecutive study, many are the mile posts that we can introduce that may not be ineffective in moulding character.

The American haste and impatience to have quick results are responsible for many a vocal catastrophe. In my long European residence, we were constantly appealed to aid students who had come over with an insufficient sum of money to be able to finish their studies. The "*step lively*" of the New York traffic manager will not apply to the European operatic impressario. He demands great perfection which, under the happiest circumstances, can only be acquired after long, quiet, conscientious and intelligent work.

Miss Fanny Reed, an American, who had practically lived all her life in Europe, and who was one of the greatest amateur artists in the world, told me that she positively dreaded to have a letter from some friend in America asking her to hear a girl sing and give her advice. She said that no matter how beautiful the voice was naturally, there was always so much to do; and the girl, very far from being an artist, she felt compelled to tell her the truth in order to really help her. Almost invariably the girl resented this criticism and said that everybody, including her professors, found her nearly ready for a debut.

Miss Reed said they never took her

advice, but about two years later they came back broken in spirit; broken in purse; and often, but not always, humbled in mind; and begged for advice, and above all for material assistance. This, she said, had kept her poor all her life.

The banks of the Seine have been strewn with these wrecks for years, and certainly there must be some national defect which produces this condition.

I believe it is largely due to the lack of understanding of the requirements necessary to become an artist, and a mistaken estimate of time and money.

VI

VOCALIZING
(*Continued*)

ALL of vocalizing has not been mastered until the trill has been acquired; and what a bugbear it is to the average person. Many people possess a shake which they attempt to impose upon the public as a trill; but the public of today is not the public of twenty-five years ago, and the genuine article, as Americans say, must be handed over.

Velocity in scales must precede the accomplishment of the trill. The notes of a trill are to be sung so rapidly that unless one has already practised sufficiently to have a certain velocity, it is an arduous task. When I think how slowly and carefully the pendulum must be swung at first, and then the amount of time, patience, thought and concentration necessary to arrive at a perfect trill, I understand why so few people ever achieve it. I shall never forget the first time that I heard Madam Melba trill in a large theatre. It was in the Auditorium in Chicago. She was singing the Mad Scene from *Lucia*, and when she came to her trill, I closed my eyes and it seemed as if I were in the great forest at Fontainebleau and all the bird kingdom was celebrating. I doubt if I shall ever again hear anything so beautiful.

Madam Marchesi told me that for years Jenny Lind could not get her trill. She practised patiently and conscientiously, and was really in despair. One summer morning, seated in her garden, a bird began trilling in the tree above. She looked up and saw his throat palpitating with a joyous sound which she tried to imitate. Her effort was crowned with success, and from that day on her trill was the envy of her compeers.

I do not for a moment believe that she could have accomplished this prowess if she had not done all the preliminary work. As a matter of fact, all her vocal organism was so trained and ready that it only required the spark of inspiration that her feathered rival furnished. Once again we find our greatest good in all that brings us in close proximity to nature—nearness to God.

Madam Marchesi had great success in teaching the trill. She had what she called her slow trill and her fast trill. For the slow, she always began in the middle register and then descended a half step and then ascended a whole step, giving the full interval. It is so much easier for a voice to trill or shake, if you will, on the semitone, but to have the pulsations absolutely even and perfect upon the larger interval requires painstaking work.

Madam Lilli Lehman, I believe, on the contrary, always begins on the upper of the two notes. In either event, the note to receive the strong accent is the top note; and at all times, with the trill I have found the pupils who achieved it the most rapidly were those who told me they felt as if they sung it almost or just back of the nose. As a matter of fact, you are singing a whole interval, but the first note is placed so high that you have the sensation that you are singing your low note too high.

Happy illusion! Hold on to it!

If the larynx has acquired a sufficient amount of agility to produce a correct trill, you can crescendo and decresendo at will.

With the field of preparatory vocalizing well under way, we now must take one of the most serious steps in a singer's whole career—the application of words to the music. If you have faithfully prepared each step of the way, as laid down in this very imperfect thesis, you will not have the same difficulty that confronts the student whose voice is placed in an inferior manner. If one would only realize that a word sung is only a word vocalized, or musicalized. It should not be so difficult. Nature has provided us so marvelously with the weapons necessary to weld the two that the voice once posed and the theme studied and understood, the task is light.

I always prefer to begin my pupils with Italian, and, in fact, I prefer for one year, at least, they sing no other language. But it is seldom that I can carry out my wishes in this respect, for so few foreigners understand Italian that they tire singing continually in a language that is to them unknown. But those who do always have the reward double fold.

"The Reason?"

Well, this is my reason—the words

of the Italian language are always
open and mellow and the constant
use of their vowels has a tendency to
keep the throat open; whereas the
French has many closed vowels, and
the German gutteral sounds. What
nature gives to the Italians the rest
of us poor mortals have to spend
years in attaining, and we never gain
the same results. Then, too, in Italian, the adjectives and articles all
have the same termination as the
noun: for instance: *La—Tua—Vita
e la mia—Povero Edgardo e morto.*

The Italians teach us the connec-
tion of the vowels and the French
the use and value of the nasal tone,
but this must always be correctly
understood and not abused. To the
Germans, I think, we must accord
the power of great expression. Is

[85]

there anything in the whole gamut of the vocal art which gives us greater pleasure than to have clear distinct diction? The actual value of the so-called ordinary diction teacher is for me a very perplexed question; and yet when one is to learn to sing in a foreign language, it is absolutely essential. I have frequently found these diction teachers demanding all kinds of lip gymnastics for the pronunciation of different sounds which were quite unnecessary and contrary to all that I had tried to instill of simplicity in emission. And it is only when a pupil has understood that she can pronounce all five vowels with the same relaxed easy, open throat that she can then study diction to advantage. So much of diction today calls for distorted faces and muscular contortion. These may be poor diction teachers, or they may have been stupid pupils; that I cannot say, but I have encountered so much of it in my work that it has made me more or less skeptical. I have had pupils so occupied with the position they must put their lips and face muscles in, that the entire thought or sentiment of the word to be conveyed was lost.

In Paris, I had a teacher, Madam Rochefort, for French diction, who was perfectly marvelous. She never found it necessary to sacrifice the tone for the word and she would take a girl with the most pronounced Western twang, and given time enough, would make her sing French like a native. She always used to say to me, "It is so easy to teach your

pupils, for the voice is all there and
it is only waiting and ready to receive
its word coloring."

Oh, my friends; think what it means
to color the tone, to be able to express one's soul, and, better still, the
soul of others through the medium of
tone and word. The fine perception
necessary to discern and know the
value of the important word in each
phrase; the word whose color gives
illumination to the whole sentence.
Many of the great dramatic artists
who have studied years and attained
a perfect diction cannot sit through
an opera. This is true of Monsieur
Mounet-Sully, Doyen of *La Comedie
Française*. He told me that he
thought the beauty of sublime sentiment entirely lost when one must
submit to hearing a well-known text

battered and torn in order that some man or woman may hold on to a note sufficiently long to procure a pyrotechnical effect. Monsieur Mounet-Sully is now over seventy years old, and only about seven years ago he was gracious enough to come and recite for me at one of my matinees.

I gave *La Ballade du Dezesperé,* words by Henri Murger and the music of Herman Bemberg, who has written so many charming French ballads. I had a string quartet of violins and 'cello and Monsieur Bemberg was at the piano. Madam Beriza sang the part of the wraith and Monsieur Mounet-Sully recited the part of the Poet who asks entrance. It is a very wonderful composition and I am certain when they had finished there was not a dry eye in the

[89]

house. Beautiful as the music is, the pathos and soul Monsieur Mounet-Sully put into his simple recitation was the thing which reached the heart and held all hearers spellbound. But that is just the point I would wish to make. Shakespeare has told us that "music soothes the savage ear," and I think we are all ready to admit the power it has to stir our emotions. This being true, then the singer has such a tremendous advantage to start with.

God has endowed him with his most perfect gifts; Nature has provided him with the means of expression; then why not endeavor to realize through the *word* medium—to paint the picture so clearly that even the deaf may hear and the blind may see.

Each word has its value; each line

its message; and none of the modern
writers has better understood how to
wed the two than Monsieur Claude
Debussy in his *Pelleas et Meli-
sande*. Many musicians consider this
opera to be the most perfect welding
of tone and word that has ever been
produced, and if the opera were to be
given with imperfect diction I can
easily believe it would lose much of
its beauty, and I doubt, in fact, if it
could carry its message.

But how acquire a perfect diction
and render supple jaw, tongue and
lips? These are all daily problems
to be met and conquered.

We have much to be grateful for,
that in Nature, supreme creation,
every want, every need has been
attended to, and if we come to our
work with an open receptive mind,

it is certain that our work is far easier. Relaxed mind, relaxed body and cheerful heart, these are the remedies I would recommend to a beginner.

VII

RESONANCE

IN the various steps of the vocal
ladder which I have endeavored
to indicate to you, perhaps none
is more discussed and sought after
than resonance; and, in fact, to do
effective work—public work, it is a
vital essential.

Resonance is dependent upon several things. First: Breath, elasticity
of the throat and the correct use of
the muscles to give free egress to the
breath. Second: The cavities of the
face and head unobstructed.

The *fausse nasal* is absolutely necessary, and, to my mind, is one of the
surest guides in tone placing. The
nose can be used at times when notes

are rebellious; but the *fausse nasal,* which lies directly under the nose, is most important.

Many people from childhood and sometimes from birth, have an obstruction in the nose, and this removed, adds to the natural resonance. The Italians by nature have very resonant voices; their language is of great assistance. The Italian tongue has many open vowels and their constant repetition gives the voice a clear, rippling quality. The ideal tone is to have the resonance combined with the velvet in the voice. Resonance exaggerated, after a time, produces a strident hard quality; and if produced with a closed throat and pushed, it is certain to undermine the best voice in the world. I have never heard anyone who, to my mind, had the complete understanding of resonance that Madam Melba has. Each tone is like a crystal ball, and she never gives any but the keenest pleasure.

Histrionically and emotionally she has never given me the same delight that many other artists have, but when I listen to her I listen to a flawless voice, flawlessly produced, and my joy is unbounded.

Madam Sembrich has the combination of velvet and crystal, but she is one of the very rare coloratura singers who does possess the two qualities.

Again recurs the question of a relaxed breath. If the breath is tight and held, the tone is certain to lack in its quota of overtones, and the resonance reduced.

Many times, teachers confine themselves to the use of the vowel *E*, the most closed of all the vowels. If the throat is open with the closed *E*, it sometimes is useful to teach one where one should feel the resonance. Sensation must come to our aid, together with hearing, if we are to have an established principle; in my own work I make use of all the different vowels, and I find that in most cases the *Ah* is the last to be really well sung. A teacher must become her own judge in employing the vowels, corresponding to the need of the pupil. If the voice is placed only on one vowel, necessarily the use of the other vowels met with in words are disturbing: the throat seems to have so adjusted itself to that one vowel that when forced to use the other vowels in the pronunciation of words, the result is often very unfortunate.

Some years ago, I had a pupil, a French woman, named Mdlle. Verna. After studying with me for four seasons, her voice became very beautiful; and when Monsieur Van Dyke heard her sing the part of the Shepherd to his *Tannhäuser*, he turned and looked up at her, which is contrary, I believe, to the tradition of the opera. As you will remember, there is no orchestra, and the note must be taken alone, and it is seldom one is absolutely on the pitch. He afterwards told Monsieur Gainsbourg, the manager of the opera house, that he had never heard such a beautiful emission of voice; and when that note rang so true, clear and pure, he forgot everything and just turned about to see who it was. As a matter of fact, Monsieur Van Dyke had never rehearsed with the company and so was unprepared for what he heard. He became so interested in this young singer, that he afterwards offered to coach her in the Wagnerian Operas; but I regret to say that she did not avail herself of this rare opportunity and another fate deprived the world of what should have been one of its best artists.

You will all know Mrs. George R. Sheldon through her noble work for the reorganization of the New York Philharmonic Society. She came to my studio, one day in Paris, to hear Mdlle. Verna sing. She was very much impressed, and afterwards sent me a most beautiful gift, accompanied by the following letter:

Hotel Ritz,
Place Vendome,
Paris.

My dear Mrs. Duff: I have had at your home today one of the rare treats of my life. The beautiful voice, the colour, the temperament are all God given, but what you have done is so wonderful, so perfect in its deep intellectual understanding that I cannot resist writing you and telling you what a gratification to you to be able to show such results. It mitigates the failures which we all feel that we have made. You are the ideal teacher. You deserve all possible praise and I have never heard the two great Schools more wonderfully combined than I have in your pupil, and which is the reflection of your brains.

Thank you for it all—it's a privilege to be called your friend.

Faithfully yours,
Mary R. Sheldon.

Dec. 14, 1907.

Madam Nordica had heard of this girl, and said to me that she wanted to hear her sing. Somehow, it never seemed to come about very easily; it was in the summer, and we were each, more or less, away from Paris. In the autumn, however, just before the day she was sailing for America, she sent me a telegram asking me if I would bring Mdlle. Verna that evening to sing for her.

We arrived at nine o'clock, and she had not yet dined. She hurried and came in to listen. Her trunks were not yet finished, and all were saying: "But don't be long, Madam; we must have your orders."

Her accompanist was there and played; Mdlle. Verna singing first the air from *Sigurd*. I saw Madam Nordica begin quite unconsciously to nod in approval, and when the girl had finished she jumped to her feet, came over and put her arms about her and said: "Thank God, to find someone who can sing E with an open throat."

Then with that genuine enthusiasm which was so characteristic, she examined her breath, jaw, etc. When she had finished she asked Mdlle. Verna to sing several pages from the opera of *Tosca*, which she did. After this, Madam Nordica came to the piano and asked her to do a few octaves, at which she said: "Where did you get all this?"

Turning to me she said: "You told me that I was to hear a pupil; I have not; on the contrary, I have listened to a finished artist. She only has to step on to the boards, and she is made."

The *A* and *E* are the clear bright vowels, and must be sung with almost a smiling mouth. *U* and *O* are dark vowels, and the lips are drawn more into a tube shape. It is not alone in singing that all these points should be employed, but also with the speaking voice.

In talking with Jean de Reszke about a pupil of his, a tenor, who had a glorious voice but never really did learn to produce it well, he said: "Why, chère Madame, how can he? He comes to me on an average of three one half hours a week, and all the rest of the time he is talking in an appalling manner; no voice can resist that treatment." The correlation of speaking and the singing voice is not placed at its proper valuation. A little care and attention when children are small, and many a pitfall can be averted.

Mme. Marchesi had a theory that the reason there were so few really beautiful singing voices among the English people, was that they were taught from the cradle to suppress the voice and speak in such a low voice; whereas the French and Americans speak in a nasal voice. The worst speaking voice in the world is the uncultured throaty voice, and it is this type of voice which frequently deters progress. If one would be an artist, one should try to place the speaking voice, as well as the singing.

VIII

MY FIRST PUPIL

MARY GARDEN! What a name to conjure with? What lover of opera has not heard, or heard of this famous artist? America claims and loves her, but Aberdeen, Scotland, was the place of her birth. When she was only six years of age her parents came to America to live and it is in this country that she grew up and received her early education. How many times I have been asked the question—''Do tell me something about Mary Garden! What was she like as a child?'' That is at once a pleasant and a complex task, for no one who did not know her as a little child will be able to understand the

To my friend Mrs Duff. Of all
my friends, the first.
Mary Garden.

MARY GARDEN

great personality she already pos-
sessed, when, as a very little girl, she
first came to see me.

After some years of study in Europe
I went to Chicago to begin my career
as a teacher of singing. Among the
many letters of introduction was one
to Mr. Robert D. Garden, Mary
Garden's father. Some weeks after
my arrival Mr. Garden came to me
one day and asked if I would be will-
ing to hear his little girl sing. He said
she had a very pretty voice and sang
frequently in Sunday School, where
she appeared to have considerable
success. Naturally I told him I would
hear her with the greatest of pleasure,
and the vision of that pretty, attrac-
tive little girl, with her gown above
her shoetops and her hair in braids
down her back, will remain indelible

in my memory. She entered the room with the composure of a woman of the world, and yet with modesty, and a complete lack of all self-consciousness. After a few moments' conversation I asked her if she would sing for me and if she could accompany herself, or if she would prefer I play for her. She immediately seated herself at the piano, played her own accompaniment, and in a delightful manner, sang for me Meyer-Helmund's *Margherita* followed by *Annie Laurie.* It is no exaggeration to say that she sang then with the same astounding musical understanding and remarkable phrasing which has colored her entire career.

Mary Garden is one of the *born* artists, for her artistic instincts were as dominant in her early years as they are today, and she possesses that incomparable art, which if not endowed by nature, can never be developed except in counterfeit form. She had infinite charm and great intelligence, and I soon became convinced that she was destined to make a career. Her voice at that time was small but very lovely and pure in quality. She began to study with me, and was, in fact, my first pupil. Her progress was marked from the very first day, and I can never remember her coming to me without knowing her lesson. When she arrived at the stage of her studies where she began to sing vocalises, she always learned and sang them by heart, and you may say that this keen attention to her work has been the keynote of her success.

After studying several years with me I realized that for her artistic development and acquiring of the languages, Chicago was no longer the desired field. Her voice had developed tremendously and all the difficulties of execution seemed eliminated. Paris was decided upon as the most desirable place for work and subsequent years have well demonstrated the wisdom of that decision. Miss Garden went over with me in May and sang before several of the greatest artists in the world, who, without exception, pronounced her voice the purest that they had ever heard. That autumn I returned to resume my work in America whilst Miss Garden remained in Paris, began her studies of the languages and continued with her vocal work.

After several years of more or less good work Miss Garden decided that she must debut and it was at Madam Sibyl Sanderson's that Monsieur Albert Carré, director of the Opéra Comique, first heard Miss Garden sing. It was quite *au-hazard* that they met there, and curiously enough, she accompanied herself at the piano and sang *La Gavotte de Manon* and *Annie Laurie*, the same song with which she had won my heart and admiration some years previous. Monsieur Carré at once recognized the great possibilities of this young woman and on the spot engaged her for two years, to sing leading roles at the Opéra Comique. That was the year that Charpentier brought out his *Louise*, the leading role of which was created by Mademoiselle

Rioton. The Opera gripped at the very hearts of the Parisians, and "standing room" only was the daily bulletin at the Comique. At the very height of this great success Mademoiselle Rioton contracted a severe cold and in spite of her most courageous efforts, her voice gave out in the middle of a performance and she was unable to go on with the role. Monsieur Carré, with his unerring judgment in all that concerned his theatre, realized that this might occur and he sent out messengers in different directions to find Miss Garden and have her in the theatre. At the end of the second act Mademoiselle Rioton announced her inability to continue the representation. Monsieur Charpentier was in the audience and when Monsieur Carré told him that Miss Garden would finish the performance he became very much excited and said ''No, this I will never permit.'' Monsieur André Messager, the Chef d'Orchestre, upheld Charpentier in his decision and declared it madness, for Miss Garden had never had a rehearsal. Monsieur Carré, exercising his authority, said *"Je suis le maître ici* (I am the master here) and the Opera will go on and will be sung by Miss Garden.'' Whereupon he stepped before the footlights, announced the illness of Mademoiselle Rioton and said that Miss Mary Garden, a young debutante, would finish the Opera.

The usual murmur of dissatisfaction at the appearance of an intruder ceased only when the curtain was rolled up on the third act and Miss

Garden, clad in an ill-fitting gown, stepped upon the stage without having had a moment's rehearsal either with the orchestra or with any of the artists. That night Mary Garden sang herself into the hearts of the Parisian public. Before the evening was over, I might almost say at the end of the great air *Depuis le Jour*, she held her audience and from then until the end of the Opera the full hearted enthusiasm of discriminating listeners became more and more pronounced. The next morning Paris awoke to the knowledge that a new star had arisen, and Mary Garden found herself heralded as a great artist.

For those who will heed there is a wonderful lesson to be gained from all this. When Miss Garden was engaged by Monsieur Carré she was told that she could understudy *Louise* and *possibly* she *might* sing it one day. Mademoiselle Rioton was at the height of her success, and to all intents and purposes, this possibility was so remote that the average young singer would have taken her time in preparing the rôle. Not so, Mary Garden. She began at once the study of the rôle and had so perfected it that when called upon *a l'improvise* she was letter-perfect and stepped in a night from the obscurity of the student life to the Premiere of one of the leading theatres of the world.

www.ingramcontent.com/pod-product-compliance
Lightning Source LLC
Chambersburg PA
CBHW020656180626
46816CB00003B/1314